This book belongs

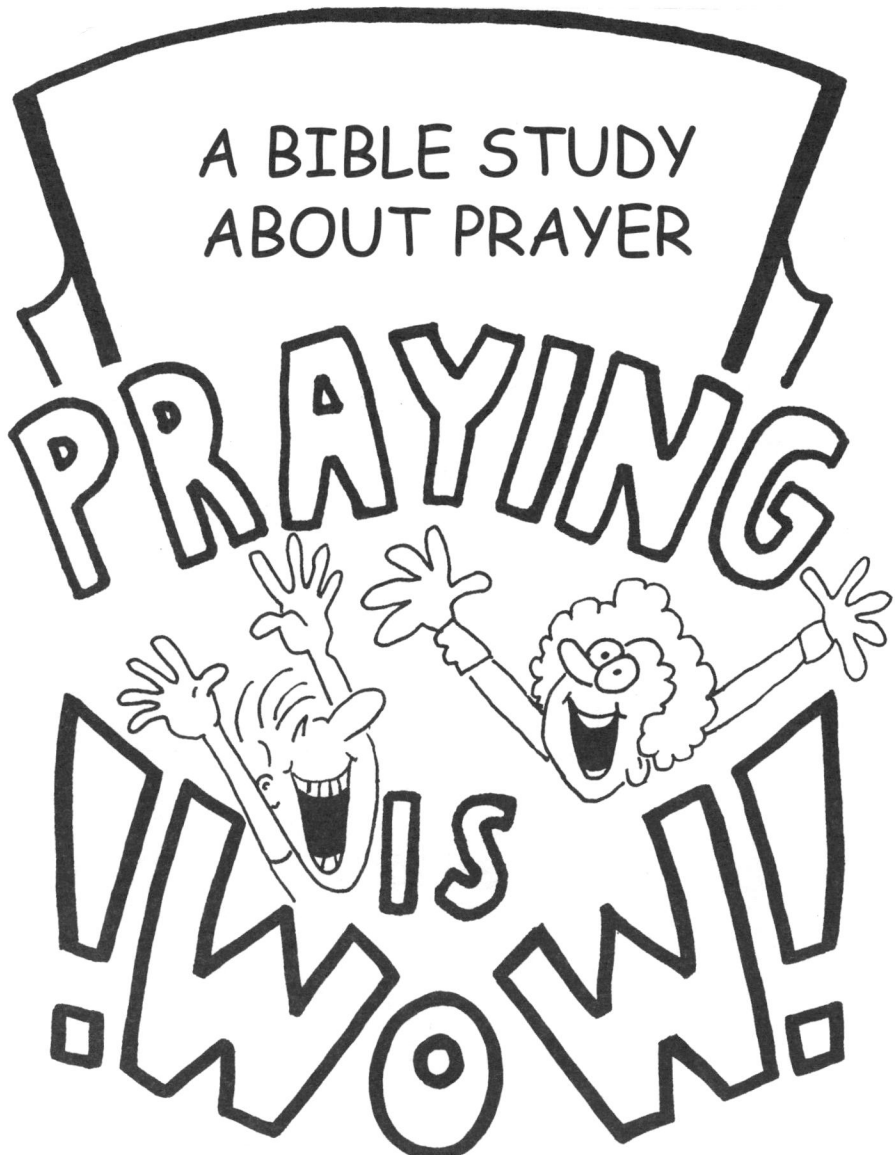

A BIBLE STUDY ABOUT PRAYER

PRAYING IS WOW!

FOR KIDS BETWEEN AGES EIGHT AND TWELVE

PRAYING is !WOW!

A Bible study about prayer
for kids between eight and twelve

Penny Elliott

Published by CHRISTIAN ART PUBLISHERS
PO Box 1599, Vereeniging 1930

© 2000 Christian Art Publishers

First edition 2000

Scripture paraphrased from:
① The *Holy Bible*, New International Version®. NIV®.
Copyright © 1973, 1978, 1984 by International Bible Society.
Used by permission of Zondervan Publishing House.
All rights reserved.
② *The Living Bible*, copyright © 1971. Used by permission of
Tyndale House Publishers Inc., Wheaton,
Illinois 60189. All rights reserved.
③ The *Holy Bible*, New King James Version.
Copyright © 1979, 1980, 1982 by Thomas Nelson
Publishers, Inc. Used by permission. All rights reserved.

Some ideas for *Praying is !WOW!* were inspired
by the reading of the book *Bill Hogg's
Most Excellent Guide to Praying* by Bill Hogg.

Cover designed by Christian Art Publishers

Printed and bound by Creda Communications

ISBN 1-86852-724-7

© All rights reserved. No part of this book may be reproduced in
any form without permission in writing from the publisher, except
in the case of brief quotations in critical articles or reviews.

02 03 04 05 06 07 08 09 10 11 - 11 10 9 8 7 6 5 4 3 2

This BIBLE STUDY is not JUST for fun!
Before you get down to work make sure that:

↳ you really WANT to learn more about PRAYING; and
↳ you are willing to make TIME each day to do this study.

REMEMBER: PRAYER AND BIBLE READING SHOULD BE A PART OF EVERY DAY.
You can use this Bible study in your special time with God each day.

 In the middle of this book you will find a PRAYER CHART. There are instructions on how to use it.

YOU WILL NEED: Find one that is easy for you to understand. BIBLE   NOTEBOOK 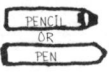 PENCIL OR PEN

L👀K OUT FOR THESE SIGNS:

 Shows you what day you're on.

 Read chapter verse — Read this first.

This arrow from the "Bible" shows where the verse is mentioned on the page.

Dear God
I may not know much about praying right now but I WANT to learn more. Help me to spend time each day going through this book. Show me how EXCITING it is to pray! In Jesus' name.
Amen.

A SPECIAL FRIEND

DAY 1

Read Exodus chapter 33 verse 11

Do you have a special friend?
If you don't, then imagine that you do!
Draw a picture of your friend's face below.

My best friend is ....

What do you like about your friend?

How often do you see your friend?

What do you talk about?

DID YOU READ YOUR BIBLE VERSE?

Who came to speak to Moses? _ _ _.
The Bible says that God spoke to Moses as a _ _ _ speaks with a _ _ _ _ _ _.
L👀K at some of the things you wrote about your best friend. Do you think you would write the same things about yourself and God?
Would you like to have God as YOUR SPECIAL FRIEND? During our next few days together we'll find out how you can.

Read Isaiah chapter 59 verse 2

SIN

DAY 3

God is holy.
Read Leviticus 11:44. What do you think this means?
....

Because God is holy He doesn't like SIN.
What is SIN? ....
Sin is something everyone has done. (Read Romans 3:23.)

○ Circle the words that have something to do with SIN:

STEALING   LOVE   LIES   CHEATING   KINDNESS
DISOBEDIENCE   WATCHING T.V.   TELLING TALES
ANGER

What does SIN do to us and God?..
....

The rectangles below are like bricks in a wall.
Inside each one write something you do that separates you from God.

How do you think God feels when you sin? Draw His face in the circle below.

Draw yourself below.

GOD   MY SINS   ME

Because of the wall of sin between you and God,
HE CANNOT HEAR YOU!
Tomorrow we'll find out how to break down the wall.
(You can look now if you can't wait!)

DAY 4: BREAK DOWN THE WALL

Read 1 John chapter 1 verse 9

SIN doesn't make God happy – does it?
God made a plan to break down the WALL of sin between us and Him.

God's PLAN was ○○○
(Read Matthew 1:21.)

...to..........................
....

What does it mean to save someone?
....

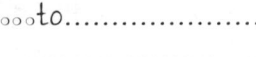

Read Colossians 2:13-14 to find out what Jesus did with our sins:
....
....

Do you also want your sins nailed to the cross? This happens when you CONFESS your sins to God, and **CRASH** the wall between you and God comes tumbling down!

YOU NEED TO PRAY:
① Tell God that you have sinned. Name your sins.
② Tell God you are sorry for these sins. Ask Him to help you not to do them again.
③ Thank God that He sent Jesus to take away your sins when He died on the cross.
④ Thank God that He has forgiven you and washed away your sins.

HERE'S WHAT YOU MUST DO! (This is also how God will become your friend!)

Do you know WHO you are now? GOD'S FRIEND!
You are a CHRISTIAN!
You are a CHILD OF GOD!
CONGRATULATIONS!
If you prayed a prayer like this before you CAN do it again. You can also just THANK GOD for what He did for you then.

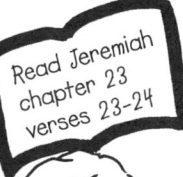

HELLO GOD! ARE YOU THERE?

Read Jeremiah chapter 23 verses 23-24

DAY 5

It's great to know that you are now A FRIEND OF GOD!

Friends love to TALK to each other.
Telephones are wonderful inventions (especially for friends!). Cellular telephones are amazing! You can use them wherever you are BUT there are still some problems.
Follow the telephone cords to find out what some of these problems are.

Can't speak long. Got to rush off!

No answer.

The answering machine speaks to you!

Someone else is speaking on the line.

Another word that means that God is everywhere all at the same time is OMNIPRESENT
Whenever you want to speak to God He will ALWAYS be there ... He's waiting to hear from you RIGHT NOW! What's more ... He's NOT IN A HURRY and it DOESN'T MATTER if someone else is speaking to Him.
HE WILL ALWAYS HAVE TIME TO LISTEN TO YOU!

TALK TO HIM NOW!

DAY 6
HOW DOES GOD SPEAK?

Read 1 Samuel chapter 3 verses 3-11

Have you read the Bible verses for today? It must have been EXCITING for Samuel to actually – **HEAR GOD'S VOICE** –

Have you heard God speak to you before? How did He speak to you? ....
....

Use the code to help you to find some ways God speaks.

1	2	3	4	5	6	7	8	9	10	11	12	13	14	15	16	17	18	19	20	21	22	23	24	25	26
A	B	C	D	E	F	G	H	I	J	K	L	M	N	O	P	Q	R	S	T	U	V	W	X	Y	Z

① CREATION — Read Numbers 22:28
② DREAMS — Read Genesis 37:6-7
③ VISIONS — Read Acts 2:17
④ ANGELS — Read Luke 1:28-29
⑤ CIRCUMSTANCES — Read Revelation 3:8
⑥ THOUGHTS — Read Matthew 26:75
⑦ INNER VOICE — Read Colossians 3:15
⑧ LOUD VOICE — Read your verses for today
⑨ OTHER PEOPLE — Read 1 Corinthians 14:3
⑩ BIBLE — Read Psalm 119:105

Tomorrow we will go into more detail...

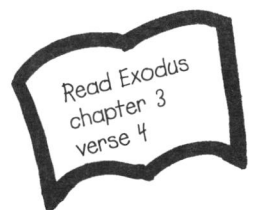 Read Exodus chapter 3 verse 4

SOME EXAMPLES

 DAY 7

Let's L**oo**k at some ways God may speak to you in more detail.

L**oo**k at the NUMBERS in the circles from yesterday's exercise and write the matching words in the spaces.

A ③ _ _ _ _ _ _ _ _ _ This is like watching a TV in your mind. Close your eyes and imagine you see a GREAT **BIG PINK ELEPHANT** riding a very small bicycle! Can you see it? Draw it in the TV set. That's what it's like when you see a vision.

God may speak to you as you read a Bible verse. Read this verse. → What does God tell you? ....
....

_ _ _ _ _ _ ⑩ **B**
Read 1 John
chapter 4
verse 21

C ⑦ _ _ _ _ _ _ _ _ _ _ _ This is like your conscience.
≥ **I know it's right** ≤   You KNOW inside of you what you have to do.

You may ask God to show you how you can help someone.
Then you have a wonderful idea (or thought) BUT you ask yourself: "Is this from God or me?" It was _ _ _ !

_ _ _ _ _ _ _ _ ⑥ **D**

I must help her weed her garden.

WHAT GOD SAYS MUST ALWAYS AGREE WITH THE BIBLE OR WHAT GOD IS LIKE.

DAY 8
HOW TO LISTEN

Read Psalms chapter 40 verse 1

To really listen to your FRIENDS speaking you have to CONCENTRATE on what they are saying. You have to STOP THINKING about other things.

Today we are going to discuss some things we should do before we listen to God.
You don't ALWAYS have to do this, but it helps.

1 TUNE IN

Confess any sins that separate you from God. It is IMPORTANT to ALWAYS keep the way between you and God clear. WHENEVER you realise you have done or said anything wrong, BREAK THE WALL DOWN!

2 CAPTURE YOUR THOUGHTS

You want to hear God speak to you so you need to tell your thoughts to be quiet! A good idea is to write down anything you have to plan later on. This stops you thinking about those things.

3 RESIST THE DEVIL

Read James 4:7. Resist means to stop something in its tracks and, if possible, to push it away.
Tell the devil to take his wrong thoughts away from you.

4 GIVE THE HOLY SPIRIT FULL CONTROL — Ask the Holy Spirit to come and direct your thinking. (Read Ephesians 5:18.)

5 PRAISE GOD — This helps you to concentrate on Him. It brings you closer to God. You may choose to sing a song or just speak out words of praise to Him.

6 EXPECT GOD TO SPEAK — Thank God that He WILL speak to you.

7 WAIT QUIETLY — Listen to what God says.

Often you will get a THOUGHT in your mind straight away. You need to BELIEVE that it is from God. You might think of a BIBLE VERSE – look it up. Someone's name may come to mind. Ask God what you must pray for them. You may see a picture in your mind.
GOD MAY SPEAK TO YOU IN ANY WAY.

You need to PRAY about what God told you.

God may just tell you He LOVES you. He may ask you to tell SOMEONE ELSE that too!

!IT'S EXCITING!

If you've never done this before then DO IT NOW!

GOD SAID...

Write what God said to you here.

DAY 9 — **REWIND 0 1 0**

Read Jeremiah chapter 33 verse 3

Can you see now why you need to have God as your friend?

- Praying is not just you t_ _ _ _ _ _ to God.
- God can tell you what to p_ _ _ _ for.
- Praying includes you listening to _ _ _ _ speaking.

L👀k at the pictures and write the story:

.... | .... | ....

If I pray with sin in my heart then ...

(Underline the correct answer)
... God will not hear.
... God will hear.

DID YOU KNOW?

God has His <u>own</u> telephone number!
Draw a TELEPHONE with His number written on it!
Write what the verse says below:

....
....
....

PRACTISE

Read Daniel chapter 6 verse 10

DAY 10

Think back to when you tried something new... like riding a bicycle.

- What new thing did you try to do? ....
- Did you get it right the first time? ....
- How did you go about getting better at this task? ....

❋ New things are often DIFFICULT at first. ❋

Have you ever had any of these thoughts when starting something new?

"I'll never get it right!"

"This is hard work!"

"I think I'll give up now!"

Then, after lots of P R A C T I S E - **!WOW!**
You get it right!
It doesn't seem so hard any more!
P R A Y I N G may be NEW for YOU.
How do you think P R A Y I N G will become easier for you?

....

You will need to ƎSITCAЯP (hold up to mirror).

💡 A GOOD IDEA is to start praying for a ƎLTTIL while each day until you become used to it.

DAY 11 — EXCUSES !EXCUSES!

Read Psalms chapter 5 verse 3

TIME, TIME, TIME. Our lives are often ruled by time these days.

Time is very INTERESTING.
Sometimes it seems to last FOREVER!
Sometimes it passes by so QUICKLY!

BUT if something <u>important</u> happens OR a <u>friend</u> comes to visit **THEN** we can always find some **TIME**.

When it comes to praying we're often good at finding EXCUSES

- I'M LATE!
- Not now God! I'm busy!
- Have to rush off!
- Must first watch my TV programme!
- I'm too tired God!

If YOU have made an excuse like one of these to God ...
STOP! Tell Him you're sorry.

You need to spend **TIME** with God <u>EVERY DAY</u>.
Underline the TIME of day that is best for you.

BEFORE BEFORE SCHOOL
BEFORE HOMEWORK
AFTER HOMEWORK
GOING TO SLEEP
ANOTHER TIME ....

Read 2 Timothy chapter 1 verse 3

TIME FOR GOD?

DAY 12

What a busy day you have!
Write down how much time you think you spend doing the following each day:

	hours	minutes
☐ Eating		
☐ Sleeping		
☐ Attending school		
☐ Doing homework		
☐ Household chores		
☐ Sport/other extramural activities		
☐ Reading/watching TV		
☐ Playing		
☐ Other things you HAVE to do		
☐ Other things you do for FUN!		
☐		
GRAND TOTAL		

✔ Put a TICK next to anything you **HAVE TO DO.**

👀 See how much time you spend doing **OTHER** things!

WE NEVER FOUND OUT HOW MUCH TIME YOU SPEND WITH **GOD** each day!

How much TIME would you LIKE to spend with God each day?
....

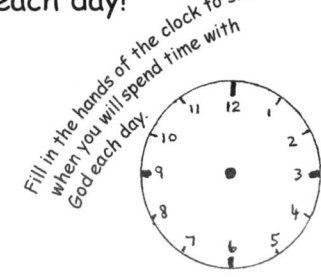

Fill in the hands of the clock to show when you will spend time with God each day.

Remember – you may have to start with a LITTLE time each day.

A SECRET MEETING PLACE

Read Matthew chapter 6 verse 6

We know that we must MEET with God daily.

It's also a good idea to find a special PLACE to meet God.

If possible you need to be AWAY from others. If you have your own room then that's probably the BEST PLACE for you.

The best place for me to MEET God is............................
....
....

DO YOU KNOW?
YOU HAVE A SPECIAL SECRET MEETING PLACE! NO ONE WILL EVER KNOW WHAT HAPPENS THERE!

Can you guess where it is? It's INSIDE of you – in your

You can be in your classroom, in a shop, walking down the street, **ANYWHERE** and God can speak to you!

These two people are meeting in a secret place.
Why?..
....
....
....
....

SHUT THE DOOR

Read 2 Corinthians chapter 10 verse 5

DAY 14

Are you in your secret place with God today?

Even though you're alone you can STILL HEAR
PEOPLE TALKING
DOGS BARKING
DOORS BANGING
THE RADIO OR TV

your mind is FULL of other thoughts.

OR you try to concentrate on God and... WOOSH!!

WHAT MUST YOU DO NOW?

You need to SHUT THE DOOR of your mind on the distractions around you and in your thoughts. You ONLY want to think thoughts that GOD GIVES.

Ask God to capture every thought that's NOT from Him.

- Close the door.
- Don't let them in.
- Tell them to stay out.
- Shut the door.

WRITE DOWN THINGS THAT DISTRACT YOU:

THESE THINGS MAY ALSO HELP:
Close your eyes.

....
....
....
....

Ask God to fill your mind with His thoughts.

Before praying, make a list of things you may need to remember later on. This should stop you planning things in your mind.

DAY 15 — NOT TOOOO COMFORTABLE!

Read 1 Kings chapter 8 verse 54

Now we're getting somewhere! We have a PLACE to pray, a TIME to pray and know what to do with our THOUGHTS.

BUT – I hope that you haven't chosen to LIE on your BED during this time.

WHAT might happen if you LIE there for TOO LONG? You may ....

You need to discover what the BEST **POSITION** is for you to be in when you PRAY.

L👀k up the Bible verses and then DRAW how the people looked when they prayed.

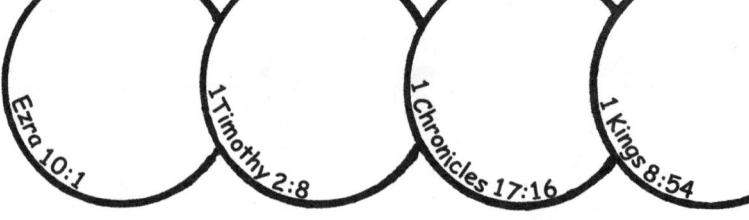

Ezra 10:1 | 1 Timothy 2:8 | 1 Chronicles 17:16 | 1 Kings 8:54

Some people like to sit at a DESK and pray. Others like to WALK and pray.

DECIDE NOW!

What (position) is the BEST ONE for you to be in when you pray?

....
....

This is me praying

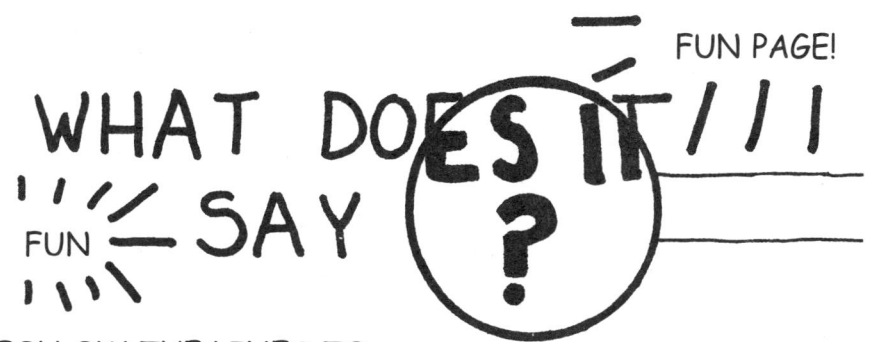

FOLLOW THE LINES TO FIND OUT WHAT THE BIBLE VERSE IS.

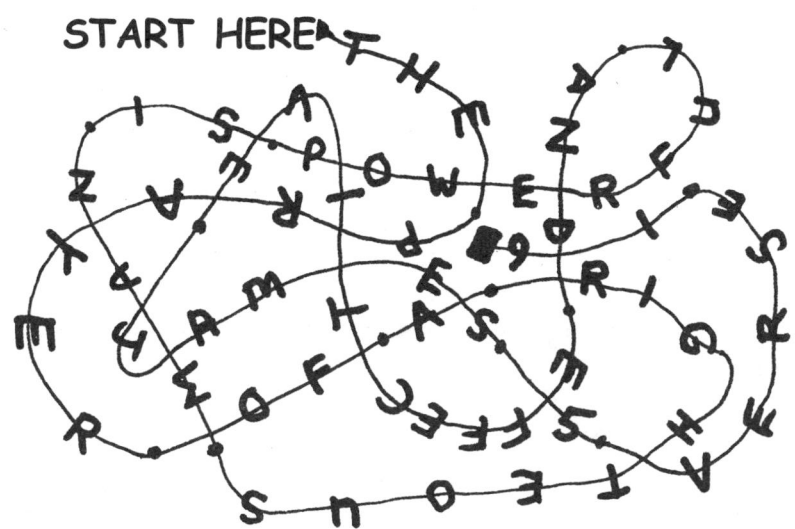

Write the verse here:

Read Psalms chapter 66 verses 18-19

Yes, I know you've heard the phrase **TUNE IN** before. You will probably hear it mentioned OFTEN.

It is **A VERY IMPORTANT** thing to do before you start to pray.

Have you ever switched on a TV set and it's been all FUZZY?
Could you see the picture CLEARLY?
What SOUND do you usually hear?

What has to be done to get the picture CLEAR?

....

When you fiddle with the knobs that TUNE the TV the PICTURE becomes CLEAR again.

Sin is like a TV set with a FUZZY picture. It gets in the way between you and God. When you TUNE IN (CONFESS YOUR SINS) the way becomes clear again.

We need to keep the way CLEAR EVERY moment of EVERY day. If you do something wrong then you should APOLOGISE to that person and to God STRAIGHT AWAY.

KEEP THE WAY CLEAR THEN YOU CAN HEAR!

Pray that the Holy Spirit will show you whenever you sin.

Do this now if you need to!

TURN THE PAGE UPSIDE DOWN TO CARRY ON!

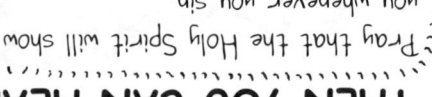 

Read Psalm chapter 8 verses 1-2

PRAISE HIM

DAY 17

A good way to start your prayer time once you've TUNED IN is to
PRAISE GOD.

PRAISE is MUCH MORE than just SINGING to God.

Did you read these verses? **!WOW!** *(Try to read this out of a NIV or Living Bible.)*
WHO praises God here? ....
HOW does praise protect you from your enemies?
....

The enemy we'd most like to see that happen to is
🐍 👄 🍎 🏃 *(Use the first letter of each picture to find out.)*
_ _ _ _ _

Psalm 22:3 in the New Kings James Version (NKJV) of the Bible says: "Yet you are enthroned as the Holy One; you are the PRAISE of Israel." Enthroned is when a ruler sits on his throne. What is the throne of God made of in this verse? ....

So, when you PRAISE God you can be sure that He is here! Your PRAISES make a throne for God to sit on!
Do you think Satan will want to stay around when you PRAISE God? _ _

PRAISE GOD FOR WHO HE IS.

You can **PRAISE** God by singing, reading Bible verses that PRAISE God (the Psalms are good to use) or just speaking out how you feel about Him.
Write down some songs you can praise God with.

1.
2.
3.
4.

DAY 18 — LOOK OUT!

Read 1 Peter chapter 5 verse 8

When we praise God we know that our enemy won't stay around ... BUT what about the REST of the time?

Satan HATES it when people want to PRAY. He doesn't mind it so much if people go to church and do good deeds.

When you PRAY he knows that the people you PRAY for are going to become CHRISTIANS and that makes him MAD!

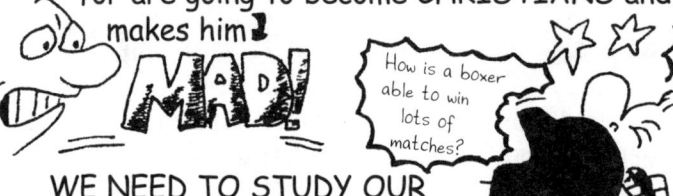

How is a boxer able to win lots of matches?

By studying his opponent and knowing his every move!

WE NEED TO STUDY OUR _ _ _ _ _ _ TOO!

▲ Read 1 Peter 5:8. What does this tell us about our enemy?..
Does it say that he IS one or IS LIKE one? _ _ _ _ _ _ _.

▲ Read the last part of John 8:44. Here we read that Satan is the FATHER of _ _ _ _ _.

He tries to make us afraid by telling us lies.

Satan is often trying to TRICK US into believing he is something he is not.
WHO IS HE REALLY?

● He is a FALLEN _ _ _ _ _ _.
● Can he be EVERYWHERE like God can? _ _
He sends his helpers (demons and evil spirits) to do his dirty work.

WE DON'T HAVE TO BE AFRAID.

We'll soon find out what God has provided for us to help us in our fight against our enemy.

Read Ephesians chapter 6 verses 11-17

YOU NEED PROTECTION

DAY 19

Some things you do every day without concentrating very much. One of those things is getting dressed. Why do you think you wear clothes every day?..................
....
What people need clothes for <u>protection</u>? ....
Let's find out about some PROTECTION God has given us.
What is it CALLED? (Read verse 11.) _ _ _ _ _ _

WE CAN PUT ON THE ...

... helmet of _____ because we are saved. It protects our minds and thoughts.

... breastplate of _____ because we are right with God. It protects our ♥s.

... belt of _____ because we know the truth about Jesus. It helps to protect us from the enemy's lies.

... shoes of _____ because we are ready to go and speak about Jesus.

We hold up the shield of _____ because we believe what the Bible says. This stops the lies of the enemy before they enter our minds.

lies of enemy fall to ground!

You need to PUT ON your **ARMOUR** every day.
The BEST TIME to do this is in the MORNING when you get dressed.
A GOOD IDEA is to PRETEND you are <u>REALLY</u> putting on each piece of ARMOUR.
As you do it you could say "I'm putting on my HELMET of SALVATION," and so on.
Now see if you can put on the rest of your ARMOUR
YOURSELF!

DAY 20 — PRAYER WEAPONS

Read Ephesians chapter 6 verses 17-18

God has given us ARMOUR to PROTECT us.
He has also provided us with WEAPONS to use.

- One of these WEAPONS is the **S** _ _ _ _ OF THE **S** _ _ _ _ _ which is really the _ _ _ _ OF _ _ _. This is the BIBLE.
  How do we use this SWORD? Matthew 4:1-11 shows us how JESUS used it.

- What 3 things did Satan ask Jesus to do?
  ....
  ....

- Each time Jesus gave the SAME reply:
  The **S** _ _ _ _ _ _ _ _ **S** say ... (Read verses 4, 7, 10.)
  THEN He quoted or repeated the Bible verse from the Old Testament to PROVE it.

- **When** Satan comes to you with his LIES like "God doesn't listen when you pray," you can tell him that it is WRITTEN in the Bible in Psalm 55:17 that He WILL hear AND answer.
  We'll have SOME **SWORD PRACTICE** soon.
  You can SEE HOW IMPORTANT it is to KNOW what is written in the Bible.

OTHER PRAYER WEAPONS ARE ...

... PRAISE (remember ...... ?)
... The BLOOD of JESUS and OUR TESTIMONY *(Read Revelation 12:11.)*
... PRAYING in the SPIRIT
(We'll talk about this another day!)

PRAYER HELPER
WHAT TO PRAY FOR:

PEOPLE WHO ARE NOT YET CHRISTIANS

- Pray that people (you too!) will tell them about Jesus.
- Ask God to send the Holy Spirit to draw the people close to Jesus.
- Pray that they will know the truth about Jesus.
- Ask the Holy Spirit to convict them of (make them aware of) their sins.
- Pray that they will read and understand what is written in the Bible.
- Pray that they'll be thirsty for Jesus.
- Pray that they'll ask God to rescue them from their sins.

PEOPLE WHO ARE CHRISTIANS

- Pray that they'll be able to share with non-Christians about Jesus.
- Pray that they'll keep the way between them and God clear so that they'll not be tempted to wander from Jesus.
- Pray that everything they do will bring praise to God.
- Pray that they will always make time to spend with Jesus.

PRAYER CHART

WHO TO PRAY FOR	MONDAY	TUESDAY	WEDNESDAY	THURSDAY	FRIDAY	SATURDAY	SUNDAY
FAMILY	Parents:	Brothers:	Sisters:	Grandparents:	Uncles/aunts:	Cousins:	Other:
FRIENDS AND OTHERS	Best friend at school:	Friend living near you:	Friend who is not a Christian:	Someone who doesn't like you:	Someone you find hard to like:	Other:	A missionary:
LEADERS	Of your country:	Principal:	Your teacher:	Another teacher:	Other:	Children's church/Sunday school teacher:	Pastor/minister:
YOUR COUNTRY	Government:	Business:	Education:	TV etc.:	Families:	Entertainment:	Church:
ANOTHER COUNTRY	Country at war:	Country with famine:	Country next to yours:	Country where no preaching is allowed:	Country with street children:	A rich country:	A poor country:
YOURSELF							
EXTRA							

HOW TO USE YOUR PRAYER CHART

This chart will help to remind you what to pray for.
The days of the week are written along the top line.
Various topics are suggested for
you to pray for under each day.
You might want to fill in a person's name under
the different headings. Write them in with pencil
then you can change them if you want to.
You will find PRAYER HELPERS in this book
that will help you to pray.

A GOOD IDEA is to have a NOTEBOOK. Write down the things God tells you to pray for. Mark them off when God answers!

PRAYER HELPER	WAR COUNTRY	FAMINE COUNTRY	COUNTRY NEAR YOU
Here are the names of some COUNTRIES you can pray for. Add in extra ones. You may choose to find them on a map. Your parents will help you!	Bosnia Angola Northern Ireland Rwanda Lebanon	Ethiopia Rwanda Sudan	
NO PREACHING IN COUNTRY	COUNTRY WITH STREET CHILDREN	RICH COUNTRY	POOR COUNTRY
Morocco Turkey Iraq Egypt North Korea Saudi Arabia	Brazil India Mexico Colombia Peru	United States Japan Great Britain France Germany	Mozambique India Romania Thailand Rwanda

PRAYER WORD SEARCH

Below is a list of words.
They all have something to do with
PRAYING!
Words are written
FORWARDS, BACKWARDS, DOWN, AND UP

on the grid below.
When you find a word, cross it off
the list.

INTERCEDE	PETITION	BEG
EARNEST	ENQUIRE	REQUEST
KNOCK	AGREE	ASK
CALL	PLEAD	SEEK

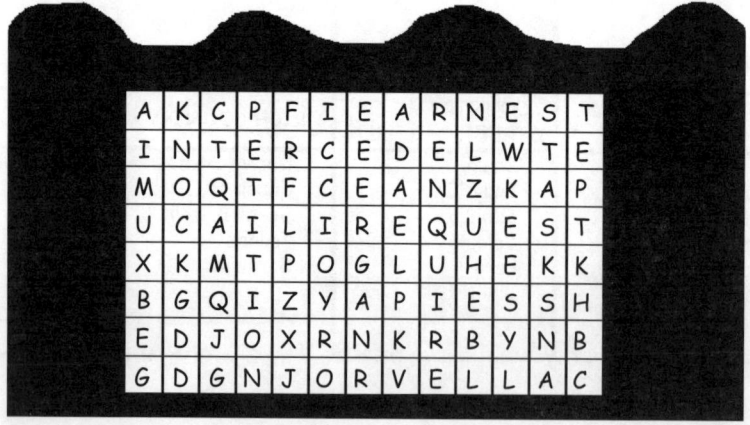

RECEIVE THE HOLY SPIRIT

DAY 21

Read John chapter 1 verses 37-39

Before JESUS died He gave His disciples, or followers, this message:

> I WILL ASK THE FATHER AND HE WILL GIVE YOU ANOTHER HELPER (THE HOLY SPIRIT).

Before JESUS was taken up to HEAVEN He said

> WHEN THE HOLY SPIRIT HAS COME UPON YOU, YOU WILL RECEIVE POWER ...

HAVE YOU EVER RECEIVED THE HOLY SPIRIT?

Some people talk about BEING BAPTISED in the Holy Spirit or BEING FILLED with the Holy Spirit.
They all mean the same thing.

HERE'S HOW **YOU** CAN RECEIVE THE HOLY SPIRIT:

- **ARE YOU THIRSTY?** — Do you WANT to receive the Holy Spirit?
- **COME TO JESUS** — Close your eyes. Concentrate on Jesus. Ask Jesus to fill you with the Holy Spirit.
- **DRINK** — Put out your hands. Imagine you are being filled to overflowing.
- **THANK AND PRAISE HIM** — Praise Jesus out loud for giving you the Holy Spirit.

!WOW! Have you RECEIVED the HOLY SPIRIT now? What happened when you received the Holy Spirit?

....

Did you FEEL anything?

....

How do you KNOW if you have received the Holy Spirit if you didn't FEEL or EXPERIENCE anything?

....

You need to **BELIEVE** that Jesus did what you asked Him to do! Tomorrow we'll find out how the Holy Spirit helps us.

DAY 22: ANOTHER LANGUAGE

Read 1 Corinthians chapter 12 verses 8-10

Yesterday you received a VALUABLE gift.
It was ....
The HOLY SPIRIT is VERY EXCITING to have around.
Have you read WHAT He wants to GIVE YOU?
One of the things He wants to give us is the ability to SPEAK in a LANGUAGE that is unknown to us. Sometimes it is called SPEAKING in TONGUES or speaking in a **PRAYER LANGUAGE**.

When we speak in a **PRAYER LANGUAGE** we SPEAK to _ _ _ (Read 1 Corinthians 14:2.)
Can we UNDERSTAND what is said? _ _
(Read 1 Corinthians 14:14.)

You CAN ask the Holy Spirit to tell you what you said.

WHY SHOULD YOU SPEAK IN A **PRAYER LANGUAGE**?
Do you often repeat the same words to God?
Do you wish you could PRAISE God more?
Have you ever wanted to PRAY and concentrate on something else at the SAME TIME?
WHEN YOU SPEAK IN A **PRAYER LANGUAGE** YOU CAN!
You may have spoken in a **PRAYER LANGAUGE** when you received the Holy Spirit.
If you didn't, then ask the Holy Spirit to give you a **PRAYER LANGUAGE** now!

DADADADA!
BABY

- ASK FOR WHAT YOU WANT!
- BELIEVE YOU HAVE RECEIVED IT!
- OPEN YOUR MOUTH!
- PRAISE GOD!

IT MAY SOUND STRANGE!
It may sound like a baby learning to talk.
Remember to PRACTISE your new language every day!

MOVING MOUNTAINS

Read Matthew chapter 21 verse 21

DAY 23

Have you ever tried to move a MOUNTAIN before?
No! Then how about remembering something VERY BIG and HEAVY that you tried to move?
Draw a picture of yourself in ACTION.

What did you have to use to help you to move this object? ....
....
....

Let's think about that MOUNTAIN again.
To be realistic – no one has ever MOVED a MOUNTAIN, have they? They may have tried to FLATTEN it or take BIG CHUNKS out of it.
What kind of equipment do they use to do this?
....
What is the EASIEST way to do this?
_ _ _ _ _ _ _ _ ! (The words are written back to front.)
WOLB TI PU

PROBLEMS can be like MOUNTAINS.

DO YOU HAVE A PROBLEM ... at home ... at school?
Whatever the problem is write it in this mountain.
How will you BLOW IT UP?

By PRAYING about it!
Tomorrow we'll find out the type of explosive to use!

DAY 24 — JUST A LITTLE!

Read Matthew chapter 17 verse 20

Before you settle down, I want you to fetch a bit of SALT or SAND. Hold it in your hand. Look at it. What is it made up of? GRAINS of ____ . Now close your eyes and imagine a MOUNTAIN. Quite a difference in SIZE, I'm sure you'll agree!

The type of explosive we use in prayer is also VERY small! What is it like? ....
Draw the smallest dot you can inside the square to see its size.

What happens to a mustard seed when it is planted and watered? ....

PRAYER **EXPLOSIVE** is called FAITH.
FAITH is BELIEVING what you know to be true.
The opposite of FAITH is D _ _ (Read James 1:5-8.)
How can we have a SEED of FAITH when praying?

- Tell God about your problem.
- Ask Him HOW you must PRAY about it.
- WAIT for Him to speak.
- He may tell you or remind you of a Bible verse that mentions your problem.
- Take the WORDS from the PROMISE given in the verse and use them in your prayer to God.

You may want to use the outline for DAY 8.

READ 1 John CHAPTER 5 VERSES 14-15

- You BELIEVE God WILL answer.
- You are praying what HE TOLD you to.
- Your FAITH starts to ....

GROW!

Read Ephesians chapter 6 verses 11-17

SWORD PRACTICE!

DAY 25

How does Satan ATTACK us?
He puts NEGATIVE THOUGHTS into our minds.
We often don't feel like PRAYING then.
We need to **CATCH** the NEGATIVE THOUGHT and stop it!
CHALLENGE it: is it from God or Satan?
CHANGE it by using your SWORD.

Satan tells you: Let's PRACTISE now!

You're afraid ...
> It is written in 2 Timothy 1:7: "For the spirit that God has given us does not make us timid (afraid); instead, His spirit fills us with power, love and self-control." THEREFORE I WILL NOT FEAR!

You can't ...
> It is written in Philippians 4:13: "FOR I CAN do everything God asks me to do with the help of Christ who gives me the strength and power." THEREFORE I CAN DO IT!

God will never forgive you ...
> It is written in 1 John 1:7 (the second part): "The blood of Jesus cleanses us from EVERY sin." THEREFORE I KNOW THAT
> ....

Complete:

No one will notice if you steal (or whatever) ...
> It is written in Jeremiah 23:24:
> " ....
> ....
> .... "

THIS IS FOR YOU TO DO YOURSELF!

PRAYER HELPER

There are many areas in your **CITY** and **COUNTRY** that influence a LOT of people. Here are some IDEAS of what you can pray for:

CHURCH
- Pray for church leaders not to be led astray by false teachings.
- Pray that they will preach only what's in the Bible.
- Pray that people belonging to churches where they are being told lies about God will find new churches.

EDUCATION
- Pray that many Christians will become teachers.
- Pray that teachers will be allowed to tell children about Jesus.
- Pray that subjects that are not godly will not be allowed to be taught.

ENTERTAINMENT
- Pray that more Christians will be involved in music, plays etc.
- Pray that entertainment which uses violence and foul language will not be popular.

TV, MAGAZINES, PAPERS
- Pray that their producers/editors will become Christians.
- Pray that they'll not allow things that don't please God to be seen by the public.
- Pray that they'll let us know about things that are important to God, like: "Abortion is wrong."

FAMILIES
- Pray that ALL family members will be honest with each other.
- Pray for protection from temptation to sin.
- Pray that all families will have houses and food to eat.
- Pray that families will spend time together.

GOVERNMENT
- Pray that Christian leaders will be elected to rule your country.
- Pray that they'll make WISE decisions.
- Pray that they'll want to please God and not just do what people want them to do.

BUSINESSES
- Pray that businesses making things that do not please God will be closed down.
- Pray that businessmen will not cheat people or tell lies just to get good deals.

"IN JESUS' NAME"

Read John chapter 14 verses 13-14

DAY 26

I bet you CANNOT count all the times you've ended a prayer with the words
BUT
DO YOU KNOW WHAT THEY MEAN?

IN JESUS' NAME Amen.

I have given the BANK a DOCUMENT. The words on this piece of paper say that MY FRIEND can DO THINGS IN MY NAME (on my behalf). This means that MY FRIEND can sign a form asking to withdraw money from my account. The bank will give MY FRIEND money from my account because I said they must.

JESUS says that we can do it too!

It is written in the BIBLE that JESUS said we can ASK ANYTHING IN HIS NAME!

The document we have is THE BIBLE.

We can sign HIS NAME on our requests to "heaven's bank." — JESUS

Have you got something special you want to ask God for? Write it here.

Prayer to the "bank of heaven": .... IN JESUS' NAME.

Pray like this: Father God, I ASK IN JESUS' NAME that you will .... because it says in the Bible .... (quote the verses mentioning the promise).

DON'T GIVE UP

Read Luke chapter 11 verses 5-10

Do you know what it means to be PERSISTENT? ....
Let's see if I can help you ...

THE PHONE RINGS... TTTRRRRR!!!! RNNGGG!!!

Won't bother to answer.

Who do they think they are!

Suppose I'd better answer.

What made the person answer the phone eventually? ....
....
THAT'S RIGHT! They were PERSISTENT!

We need to be like that when we PRAY to God. We KNOW God hears us when we PRAY but SOMETIMES He doesn't ANSWER straightaway. If this happens do you think you should:

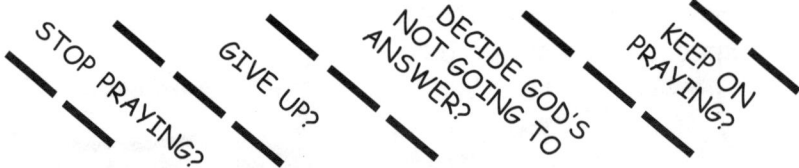

STOP PRAYING?   GIVE UP?   DECIDE GOD'S NOT GOING TO ANSWER?   KEEP ON PRAYING?

Some people have PRAYED FOR YEARS for family to become CHRISTIANS – AND THEY HAVE!
WHY? BECAUSE PEOPLE **NEVER GAVE UP** PRAYING!
We can KEEP ON PRAYING by REMINDING God of the PROMISES He gave us in His WORD.

WHO WILL PRAY?

DAY 28

Read Ezekiel chapter 22 verse 30

Can SINNERS pray? ....
Do you think that God will answer them?........................

MOST SINNERS don't WANT to pray to God ANYWAY. So how does a sinner change his mind and WANT to become a CHRISTIAN?

THEY NEED SOMEONE TO PRAY TO GOD FOR THEM.

The Bible calls this STANDING IN THE _ _ _.
What does this mean? It means that YOU take that person's PLACE and ask God to save them from their sins. When you do that YOUR PRAYERS build a BRIDGE between THEM and God.

| Sinner | GAP | God |
| Sinner | 🙏 PRAYERS | God |

Then God is able to send the Holy Spirit to make them aware of their sin!

You can **STAND IN THE GAP** for people who are SICK, SAD, IN OTHER COUNTRIES ... for **WHOEVER** or **WHATEVER**!

GOD IS LOOKING for people to **STAND IN THE GAP.**
WILL YOU?
....

| NAME OF PERSON | | God |

YOU

Draw a picture of yourself STANDING IN THE GAP for someone.

 # WHO TO PRAY FOR?

Read 1 Timothy chapter 2 verse 1

So, you're READY to PRAY now ...

But **WHO** are you going to PRAY FOR?
Use the code to help you.

□	△	I	─	○	⌀	⌀	⊞	⊠	▲	▲	▲	▲	◉	⊕	⊖	⊘	⊗	✱	⊣	⊟	⊤	⊥
A	B	C	D	E	F	G	H	I	J	K	L	M	N	O	P	Q	R	S	T	U	V	W	X	Y	Z

Join the correct Bible verse and word together.

- ○✱○⊕⊤▲▲○
  _ _ _ _ _ _ _ _

- ⊘⊟I⊠
  _ _ _ _

- ⊘□□▲○○ (I□⊕○○□▲⊘)
  _ _ _ _ _ _ _ _ _ _ _ _ _

- I□□▲─⊕○▲
  _ _ _ _ _ _ _

- ⊣⊟─▲⊣⊘
  _ _ _ _ _ _

- I□⊕○○□▲ I⊕□○▲▲○⊕○
  _ _ _ _ _ _ _ _ _ _ _ _ _ _ _ _

Acts 12:5
Matthew 19:13
1 Timothy 2:1
Isaiah 1:17
Ephesians 6:18
James 5:14

Write a prayer for one of the above.

THOSE IN AUTHORITY

DAY 30

We read in this Bible verse that we must also PRAY for THOSE IN **AUTHORITY**.

What do you think AUTHORITY means?
....

People in AUTHORITY have the right to tell us what we can and cannot do.
Someone in AUTHORITY has a BIG responsibility.

Imagine that you are the leader of a country. What kind of DECISIONS would you have to make? ....
....

You can be sure that someone in AUTHORITY needs YOUR PRAYERS! YOU can STAND IN THE GAP for them! Ask God to give them WISDOM, PROTECTION and ....

People you know that have AUTHORTIY over you are your

FATHER **MOTHER** **PRINCIPAL** **TEACHER**

People in AUTHORITY give you RULES to obey.
This is because they want to protect you.
Write the NAMES of people in AUTHORITY that you should PRAY for each day. →

Leader of country: ....
Teacher: ....
Parents: ....
Other: ....

DAY 31 — PRAY FOR THEM?

Read Luke chapter 6 verse 28

Before we begin today, I want you to think of SOMEONE that you would LOVE to see VANISH **RIGHT NOW!**

Write their name here.

WHAT has this person DONE to YOU?

- Hurt me.
- Told lies about me.
- Got me into trouble.
- Teased me.

ANYTHING ELSE? ....

The Bible says that we must _ _ _ _ for them.

We also read in Mark 11:25 that we must _ _ _ _ _ _ _ _ them.
This sounds like something we've spoken about before, doesn't it?
That's right! It's time to TUNE IN again!

We need to FORGIVE OTHERS before we PRAY.
We may not FEEL that we like the person more, BUT we can ASK God to help us change the way we think about them.

> Dear God
> I'm sorry for not liking ....
> Forgive me.
> I forgive them for ....
> ....
> Help me to LOVE them like you do.
> Amen.

If someone keeps on doing something to you that is VERY WRONG you may also want to speak to an adult you can trust about it.

Read Philippians chapter 4 verses 6-7

FOR ME TOO??

DAY 32

① Imagine that your father has been away for a long time.

② He walks in the door and your FIRST words are...

③ "WHAT DID YOU BRING ME!"

OOPS! Maybe we should have a REPLAY. Write the words here that you SHOULD have said to your dad.

④

We are often like this with God. We come to Him with a L O N G list of things that we want Him to give us ... That's why we've spoken about PRAYING FOR OTHERS **FIRST!**

God DOES want us to ask for things for ourselves too.

We can come to God when we are worried about something. He wants to take away our fears, loneliness, sadness – or whatever – and give us

.... (think of opposites).

1 Peter 5:7 also shows us what we can do.

1. Pretend to put all the things that worry you into your hands.

2. Lift your hands up high, palms turned up. Ask Jesus to take them away from you.

3. Turn your palms to face the ground. Imagine that those things go away.

4. Bring your arms down to your sides. Thank God for what He has done.

 BE A MISSIONARY NOW!

Read Matthew chapter 28 verses 18-20

What does a MISSIONARY do? ....
....

Some people KNOW that God wants them to GO to ANOTHER country and tell the people there about Jesus WHEN THEY ARE VERY YOUNG.

Did you know that **YOU** can be a MISSIONARY **NOW?**
You may be too young to GO to another country now,
BUT you **CAN PRAY** for people in other countries.

THE PEOPLE IN MANY COUNTRIES ...
...don't believe in God.
...don't allow Christians to speak about Jesus.
...are fighting each other.
...are hungry.
...believe in other gods.

These people need YOUR P _ _ _ _ _ S!

When you PRAY for other COUNTRIES and the people who live in them you are
S _ _ _ _ _ _ _ _ IN THE GAP!
Another word for this is INTERCEDING.

→ **GO NOW!**
PRAY FOR A COUNTRY.
BE A **MISSIONARY!**

ASK God WHICH country to pray for. Wait for Him to tell you. (Use Day 8 as a guideline.)
The COUNTRY I will PRAY for is
....

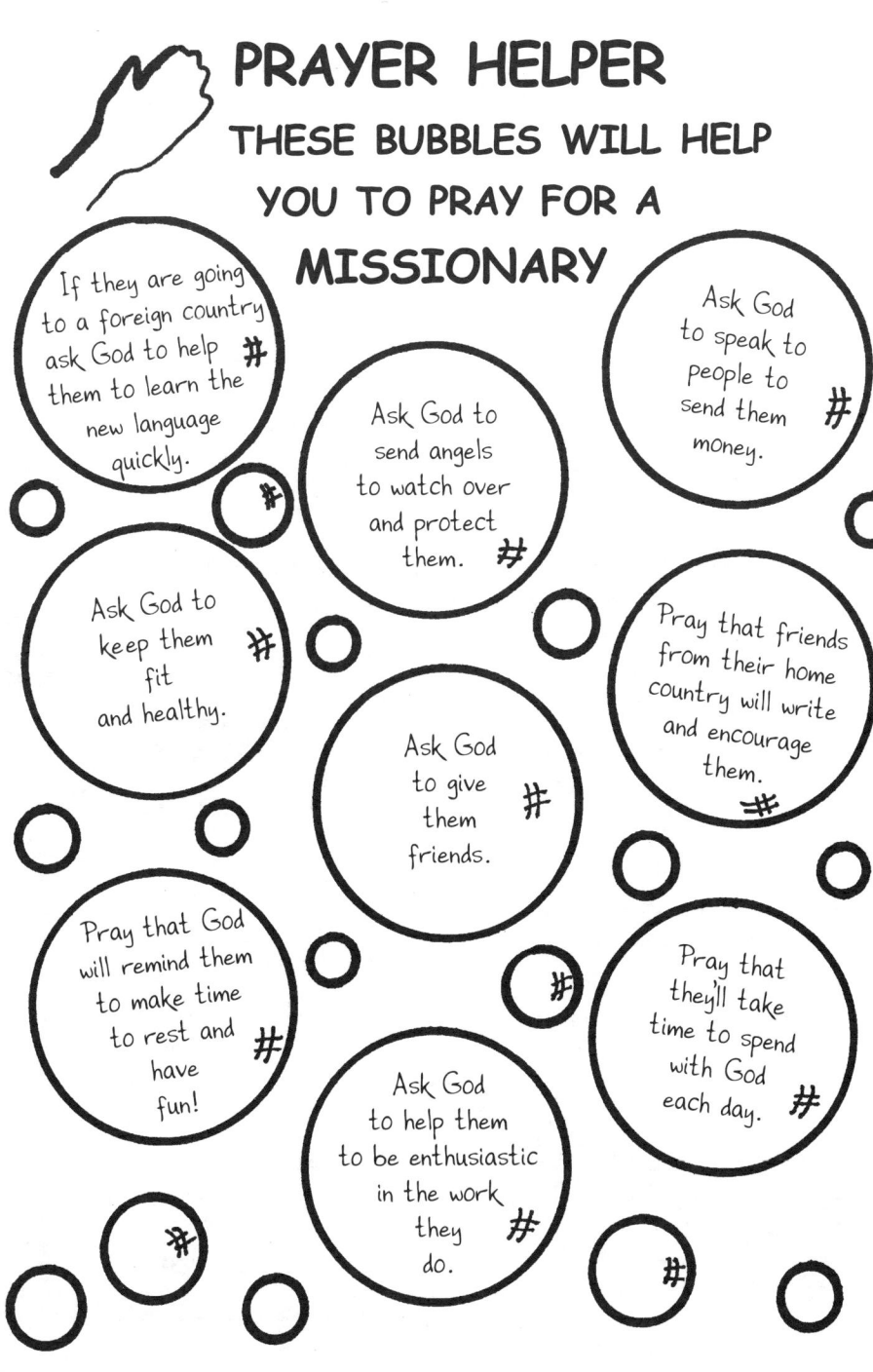

DAY 34 — AGREE

Read Matthew chapter 18 verses 19-20

Have you ever had a GOOD IDEA? Did you keep it to yourself? .... OR tell SOMEONE else? .... When we SHARE ideas with others it HELPS us to BELIEVE even MORE that it IS a GOOD IDEA.

I'm going to deliver newspapers for extra pocket money.

When we PRAY with OTHERS we can AGREE with each other's PRAYERS.

Jesus said that if _ _ _ or more **A** _ _ _ _ _ about ANYTHING you ASK FOR, His Father WILL DO IT!

I have heard about MANY PEOPLE who started PRAYING together with just ONE friend at their school. Because of this MANY children in their school became CHRISTIANS!

IDEA!

START A CLUB at your SCHOOL with CHRISTIAN friends. Meet during BREAK. PRAY for your classmates to become CHRISTIANS. EXPECT God to answer! By doing this you and your friends will be STANDING IN THE **GAP!**

Read Philippians chapter 4 verse 6

THANK YOU

DAY 35

I can recall hearing some children asking their Father:

> Dad, please can we go to the zoo? PLEASE Dad? THANKS Dad! You're SO kind!
> THANKS
> (Before Dad has even answered!)

Jesus said: "FATHER, THANK YOU for hearing me."
John 11:41

Do you think you should THANK God ...

... before He answers ?

... after He has answered ?

... before you ask ?

| WE **PRAISE** GOD FOR **WHO HE IS!** | WE **THANK** GOD FOR **WHAT HE'S DONE!** |

MY THANK YOU LIST

Let's consider some things to **THANK** God for:
... that He's heard your prayer ...
... that you don't have to carry your problems anymore ...
... for EVERYTHING He's done for YOU!

WRITE your OWN list of **THANKS** TO GOD here.
You could COUNT YOUR BLESSINGS. Think of what you have that others don't.

DAY 36 — DON'T WANDER!

Read Isaiah chapter 55 verses 8-9

It may seem at times that God doesn't **ANSWER!**

WHY IS THAT?

If we knew WHY God did or didn't do things then there would be NO NEED for God!

Sometimes God doesn't answer us because we are not praying the way we should. We need to KEEP our EYES on God and NOT WANDER OFF THE PRAYER ROAD.

Now we are going to go on a prayer journey. You will need your Bible to help you to
KEEP ON THE TRACK!

START

RULES
Follow the road to the FINISH.
If the road is BLOCKED you have to take the OTHER ROAD which takes longer.
To get back on the road you have to fill in the spaces.

DRAW YOURSELF

fiery darts of enemy

You think that God won't hear so you don't bother to pray. 1 John 5:15 says we know that God is .... and will ....

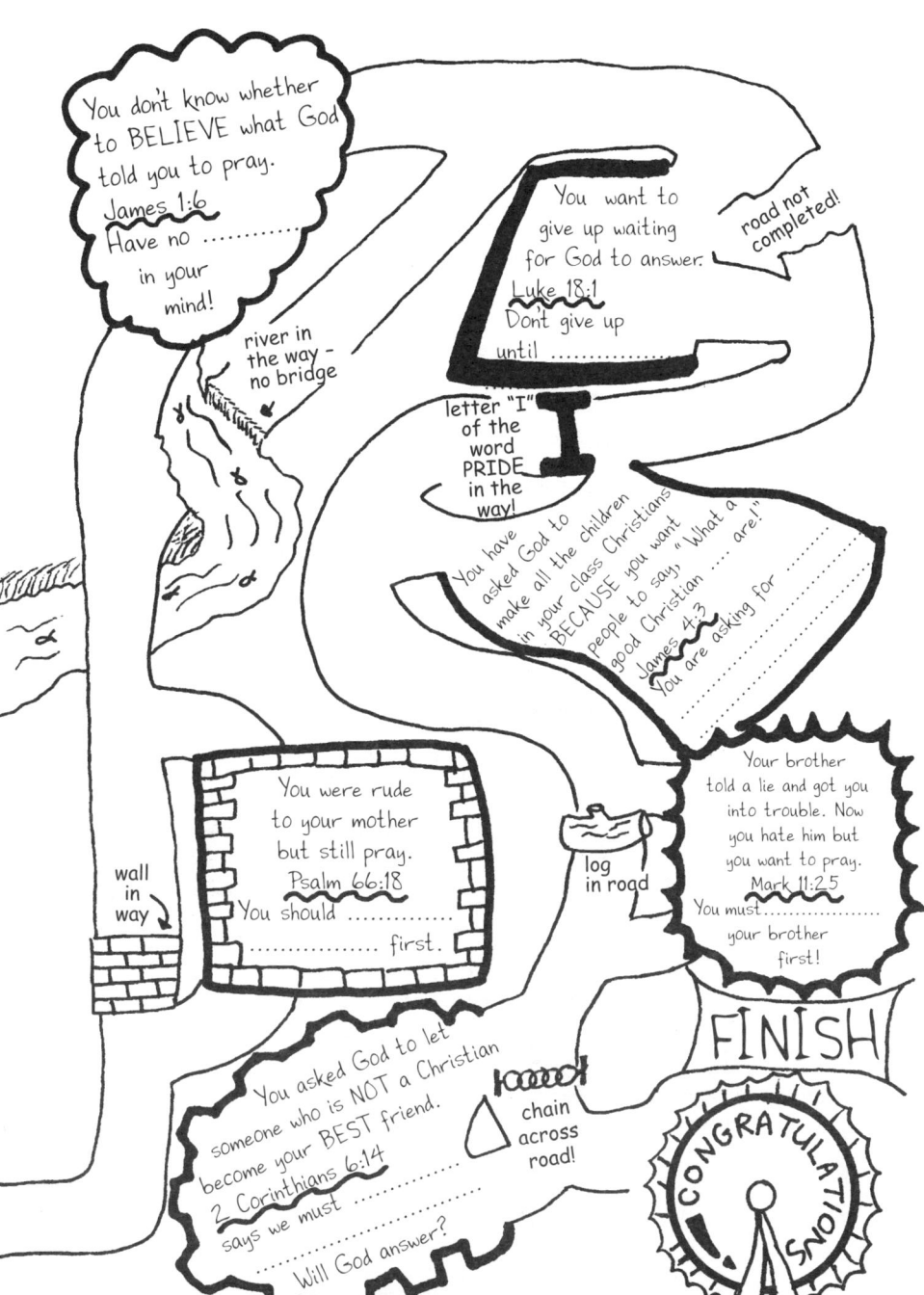

THE LORD'S PRAYER

Read Matthew chapter 6 verses 9-13

Start our time together today by saying the Lord's Prayer. I DON'T have to tell you the words because you probably KNOW them by ♡!

Did you READ what I asked you to do?
I asked you to **SAY** the Lord's Prayer.

That's what we do. We **SAY** the words but they don't mean much to us.

Jesus said: "This is how you should **PRAY**."

I should have asked you to _ _AY instead of _AY!

We are now going to take a NEW LOOK at
THE LORD'S PRAYER.
NEXT TIME you might even PRAY it
and KNOW what you're **PRAY**ING
(instead of **SAY**ING it!)

We'll L👀K at it a LITTLE piece at a time.
You could use it as a guide to help you pray.

OUR FATHER
Who do we PRAY to? _ A _ _ E _.
That makes us His <u>C</u> _ <u>I</u> _ _ _ _ <u>E</u> _.

IN HEAVEN,
This is where He _ I _ E S.
He is seated on His _ _ _ O _ E.

HALLOWED BE YOUR NAME,
This tells us that God is H _ L _.
We can come to <u>W</u> _ <u>R</u> _ <u>H</u> _ <u>P</u> Him.
He is also our SHEPHERD, ...

YOUR KINGDOM COME, YOUR WILL BE DONE ON EARTH AS IT IS IN HEAVEN.

God wants His _ I _ G _ O _ to come into people's lives. That means that they will become C _ R _ S _ I _ N _.

GIVE US TODAY OUR DAILY BREAD.

We can ask God for the things that we and others _ E E _.

FORGIVE US OUR DEBTS,

We need to C _ N _ E _ S our S _ _ S to God.

AS WE ALSO HAVE FORGIVEN OUR DEBTORS.

Read Matthew 6:14-15. For God to F _ R _ I _ E you, you have to _ O _ G _ V _ others.

AND LEAD US NOT INTO TEMPTATION,

Temptation can lead us to S _ N.

BUT DELIVER US FROM THE EVIL ONE.

What protects you from your enemy? Ephesians 6:11 says our A _ _ _ _ _ R protects us.

YOURS IS THE KINGDOM AND THE POWER AND THE GLORY.

PRAISE GOD!

AMEN !SO BE IT!

NEXT TIME - PRAY IT, DON'T SAY IT!

Read 1 John chapter 5 verses 14-15

We have discussed a lot of things about PRAYER during our time together.

Let's go through the things we've done and FIT them together.

1
To make sure that we are not wasting our time praying we need to remember to T _ _ _ I _ every day.
This keeps the 🚪 way between us and _ _ _ clear.
Then we can pray and He will L I _ _ _ _ _ .

2
PRAYING takes P R _ _ _ _ _ _ _ to get used to it.
We need to set aside a P L _ _ _ and a
🌍 T _ _ _ to pray each day.

3
We mustn't forget to put on our prayer
A R _ _ _ _ _ and take up our S _ _ _ _ _
each morning.

4
The Holy Spirit HELPS us when we don't know what to P R _ _ .
We can also pray in our own PRAYER L A _ _ _ _ _ _ _ .

REMEMBER: PRAYER **AND** BIBLE READING SHOULD BE A PART OF EVERY DAY!

5" We can pray with CONFIDENCE. We can ask God to move **PROBLEM** M O _ _ _ _ _ _ _ _ away. We BLAST our problems away with a little bit of F A _ _. FAITH grows when we pray Bible V E _ _ _ _ back to God that give us promises about our problems. We also pray in the N _ _ _ of Jesus.

6 We MUSTN'T S T _ _ praying when we have no answer straight away. We must keep on A _ _ I N G.

7" God wants us to S T _ _ _ in the G _ _ _ and pray for other people. We must pray for leaders, ...
....

HOW TO PRAY EACH DAY

- Confess any sins.
- Put on your armour if you haven't yet.
- Capture your thoughts.
- Silence Satan by your PRAISE (by singing, speaking or your prayer language).
- Ask the Holy Spirit to fill you afresh.
- Take your PRAYER CHART and ask God WHAT He wants you to pray for each person.
- WAIT for Him to speak to you.
- Write down what He says.
- Pray what HE TOLD YOU TO PRAY!
- Make note of ANY ANSWERS!

THIS IS JUST A SUGGESTION ...

QUIZ!

Here is a QUIZ! for you to do!

If you need help, LOOK at the DAY mentioned!

CLUES ACROSS:

① We need to have a special _ _ _ _ _ where we can pray (5 letters, DAY 13).

⑤ Jesus said we must pray to our _ _ _ _ _ _ (6 letters, DAY 37).

⑥ God speaks to us through His WORD which is the _ _ _ _ _ (5 letters, DAY 7).

⑧ Jesus said we can pray in His _ _ _ _ (4 letters, DAY 26).

CLUES DOWN:

① To get used to praying we need to _ _ _ _ _ _ _ _ (8 letters, DAY 10).

② Before we pray we should put on our prayer _ _ _ _ _ _ (6 letters, DAY 19).

③ Praise chases away our _ _ _ _ _ (5 letters, DAY 17).

④ A weapon we can use is the _ _ _ _ _ of the Spirit. (5 letters, DAY 20).

⑤ If we pray with a tiny seed of _ _ _ _ _ we can move problem mountains (5 letters, DAY 24).

⑦ When we pray for others we are standing in the _ _ _ (3 letters, DAY 28).

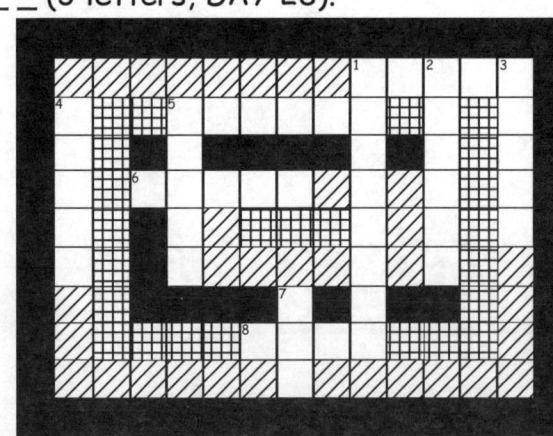